Joel Schick's
Christmas
Present

Joel Schick's Christmas Present

J. B. Lippincott Company
Philadelphia and New York

U. S. Library of Congress Cataloging in Publication Data
Schick, Joel.   Joel Schick's Christmas present.
SUMMARY: During the "twelve days of Christmas," a household receives such
monstrosities as five moldy things, six sneeds a-slavering, and ten gorks a-creeping.
1. Christmas—Juvenile poetry. [1. Christmas poetry] I. Title. II. Title: Christmas
present.   PZ8.3.S344Jo   811'.5'4   77-3236   ISBN-0-397-31761-1.

n the first day of Christmas
My true love gave to me
A partridge in a pear tree.

On the second day of Christmas
My true love gave to me
Two dorkle bugs,
And a partridge in a pear tree.

On the third day of Christmas
My true love gave to me
Three grenjikens,
Two dorkle bugs,
And a partridge in a pear tree.

On the fourth day of Christmas
My true love gave to me
Four appalling knurrs,
Three grenjikens,
Two dorkle bugs,
And a partridge in a pear tree.

On the fifth day of Christmas
My true love gave to me
Five moldy things,
Four appalling knurrs,
Three grenjikens,
Two dorkle bugs,
And a partridge in a pear tree.

On the sixth day of Christmas
My true love gave to me
Six sneeds a-slavering,
Five moldy things,
Four appalling knurrs,
Three grenjikens,
Two dorkle bugs,
And a partridge in a pear tree.

On the seventh day of Christmas
My true love gave to me
Seven swumps a-squirming,
Six sneeds a-slavering,
Five moldy things,
Four appalling knurrs,
Three grenjikens,
Two dorkle bugs,
And a partridge in a pear tree.

On the eighth day of Christmas
My true love gave to me
Eight ugly wilkings,
Seven swumps a-squirming,
Six sneeds a-slavering,
Five moldy things,
Four appalling knurrs,
Three grenjikens,
Two dorkle bugs,
And a partridge in a pear tree.

On the ninth day of Christmas
My true love gave to me
Nine lazy planzinks,
Eight ugly wilkings,
Seven swumps a-squirming,
Six sneeds a-slavering,
Five moldy things,
Four appalling knurrs,
Three grenjikens,
Two dorkle bugs,
And a partridge in a pear tree.

On the tenth day of Christmas
My true love gave to me
Ten gorks a-creeping,
Nine lazy planzinks,
Eight ugly wilkings,
Seven swumps a-squirming,
Six sneeds a-slavering,
Five moldy things,
Four appalling knurrs,
Three grenjikens,
Two dorkle bugs,
And a partridge in a pear tree.

On the eleventh day of Christmas
My true love gave to me
Eleven viperous fygreens,
Ten gorks a-creeping,
Nine lazy planzinks,
Eight ugly wilkings,
Seven swumps a-squirming,
Six sneeds a-slavering,
Five moldy things,
Four appalling knurrs,
Three grenjikens,
Two dorkle bugs,
And a partridge in a pear tree.

On the twelfth day of Christmas
My true love gave to me
Twelve grummbers grumbling,
Eleven viperous fygreens,
Ten gorks a-creeping,
Nine lazy planzinks,
Eight ugly wilkings,
Seven swumps a-squirming,
Six sneeds a-slavering,
Five moldy things,
Four appalling knurrs,
Three grenjikens,
Two dorkle bugs,

And a partridge in a pear tree.

Joel Schick has illustrated many books for children, including THE GOBBLE-UNS'LL GIT YOU EF YOU DON'T WATCH OUT! He and his wife Alice live in Monterey, Massachusetts.

The Schicks exchange Christmas presents with a dog, six cats, two gerbils, and each other.